INDEX pt I

Page(s)

8	Key
9	
10	
11	
12	28 Day Calendar
14	Weekly Reflection
16	
17	
18	28 Day Goal Setting
20	7 Day Goal Setting - Week 1
22	Week 1 Planner
24	
25	
26	Monday - Week 1, Day 1 - Morning Preparation
28	Monday - Week 1, Day 1 - Evening Review
30	Tuesday - Week 1, Day 2 - Morning Preparation
32	Tuesday - Week 1, Day 2 - Evening Review
34	Wednesday - Week 1, Day 3 - Morning Preparation
36	Wednesday - Week 1, Day 3 - Evening Review
38	Thursday - Week 1, Day 4 - Morning Preparation
40	Thursday - Week 1, Day 4 - Evening Review
42	Friday - Week 1, Day 5 - Morning Preparation
44	Friday - Week 1, Day 5 - Evening Review
46	Saturday - Week 1, Day 6 - Morning Preparation

Page(s)	
48	Saturday - Week 1, Day 6 - Evening Review
50	Sunday - Week 1, Day 7 - Morning Preparation
52	Sunday - Week 1, Day 7 - Evening Review
54	
55	Mandala
56	
57	
58	Week 1 Gratitude Log
60	Week 1 Review
62	Weekly Premeditation of Obstacles
64	Weekly Reflection
66	
67	
68	7 Day Goal Setting - Week 2
70	Week 2 Planner
72	
73	
74	Monday - Week 2, Day 1 - Morning Preparation
76	Monday - Week 2, Day 1 - Evening Review
78	Tuesday - Week 2, Day 2 - Morning Preparation
80	Tuesday - Week 2, Day 2 - Evening Review
82	Wednesday - Week 2, Day 3 - Morning Preparation
84	Wednesday - Week 2, Day 3 - Evening Review
86	Thursday - Week 2, Day 4 - Morning Preparation
88	Thursday - Week 2, Day 4 - Evening Review
90	Friday - Week 2, Day 5 - Morning Preparation

cont'd

INDEX pt II

Page(s)

92	Friday - Week 2, Day 5 - Evening Review
94	Saturday - Week 2, Day 6 - Morning Preparation
96	Saturday - Week 2, Day 6 - Evening Review
98	Sunday - Week 2, Day 7 - Morning Preparation
100	Sunday - Week 2, Day 7 - Evening Review
102	
103	Mandala
104	
105	
106	Week 2 Gratitude Log
108	Week 2 Review
110	Weekly Premeditation of Obstacles
112	Weekly Reflection
114	
115	
116	7 Day Goal Setting - Week 3
118	Week 3 Planner
120	
121	
122	Monday - Week 3, Day 1 - Morning Preparation
124	Monday - Week 3, Day 1 - Evening Review
126	Tuesday - Week 3, Day 2 - Morning Preparation
128	Tuesday - Week 3, Day 2 - Evening Review
130	Wednesday - Week 3, Day 3 - Morning Preparation

Page(s)

132	Wednesday - Week 3, Day 3 - Evening Review
134	Thursday - Week 3, Day 4 - Morning Preparation
136	Thursday - Week 3, Day 4 - Evening Review
138	Friday - Week 3, Day 5 - Morning Preparation
140	Friday - Week 3, Day 5 - Evening Review
142	Saturday - Week 3, Day 6 - Morning Preparation
144	Saturday - Week 3, Day 6 - Evening Review
146	Sunday - Week 3, Day 7 - Morning Preparation
148	Sunday - Week 3, Day 7 - Evening Review
150	
151	Mandala
152	
153	
154	Week 3 Gratitude Log
156	Week 3 Review
158	Weekly Premeditation of Obstacles
160	Weekly Reflection
162	
163	
164	7 Day Goal Setting - Week 4
166	Week 4 Planner
168	
169	
170	Monday - Week 4, Day 1 - Morning Preparation
172	Monday - Week 4, Day 1 - Evening Review
174	Tuesday - Week 4, Day 2 - Morning Preparation

cont'd

INDEX pt III

Page(s)

176	Tuesday - Week 4, Day 2 - Evening Review
178	Wednesday - Week 4, Day 3 - Morning Preparation
180	Wednesday - Week 4, Day 3 - Evening Review
182	Thursday - Week 4, Day 4 - Morning Preparation
184	Thursday - Week 4, Day 4 - Evening Review
186	Friday - Week 4, Day 5 - Morning Preparation
188	Friday - Week 4, Day 5 - Evening Review
190	Saturday - Week 4, Day 6 - Morning Preparation
192	Saturday - Week 4, Day 6 - Evening Review
194	Sunday - Week 4, Day 7 - Morning Preparation
196	Sunday - Week 4, Day 7 - Evening Review
198	
199	Mandala
200	
201	
202	Week 4 Gratitude Log
204	Week 4 Review
206	Weekly Premeditation of Obstacles
208	
209	
210	28 Day Tracking
212	28 Day Review
214	Health & Wellness Tracking
216	Meditation Guides

KEY

If you are using symbols, record them here for easy reference.

28 DAY CALENDAR

	MONDAY	TUESDAY	WEDNESDAY
WEEK 1			
WEEK 2			
WEEK 3			
WEEK 4			

THURSDAY	FRIDAY	SATURDAY	SUNDAY

"Some things are in our control and others not. Things in our control are opinion, pursuit, desire, aversion, and, in a word, whatever are our own actions. Things not in our control are body, property, reputation, command, and, in one word, whatever are not our own actions."

— Epictetus

WEEKLY REFLECTION

16

28-DAY GOAL SETTING

What are your goals? Make them specific and achievable in 28 days.

What are some likely preferred results if the goals are met?

What are some likely unpreferred results if the goals are not met?

What are the steps to take to most likely achieve the goals?

What are some obstacles that may obstruct meeting the goal?

What can you do to prepare for or reduce the chances of them happening?

What should you do if these obstacles happen?

7-DAY GOAL SETTING - WEEK 1

Review your 28-day goals. Look at the steps you should do to achieve the goals, and what you can do to reduce the chances of the obstacles you anticipated. With those in mind, what are your goals for the next 7 days? Make them specific and achievable in 7 days.

What are some likely preferred results if the goals are met?

What are some likely unpreferred results if the goals are not met?

What are the steps to take to most likely achieve the goals?

What are some obstacles that may obstruct meeting the goal?

What can you do to prepare for or reduce the chances of them happening?

What should you do if these obstacles happen?

WEEK 1 PLANNER

	Monday	Tuesday	Wednesday

	Thursday	Friday	Saturday	Sunday

24

MONDAY — WEEK 1, DAY 1
MORNING PREPARATION

How long did you sleep? Meditate ☐
(pg 216)

How well did you sleep? /5 Exercise ☐

Morning Reading:

Review your 7-day goals. With those goals in mind, make a **'Knockout List'** of 3-5 tasks you must work to complete today. Specify the tasks, and make them something you expect you can achieve today.

What are some likely preferred results if you complete these tasks?

What are some likely unpreferred results if you don't?

What is most in your control to complete these tasks?

What are some obstacles you are likely to face today?

What can you do to prepare for or reduce the chances of them happening?

What should you do if these obstacles happen?

> *"You have power over your mind — not outside events. Realize this, and you will find strength."*
> — Marcus Aurelius

EVENING REVIEW

BREAKFAST	LUNCH	SUPPER	SNACKS

What were the most significant obstacles you faced today?

How could these obstacles have been worse?

How did you or how can you mitigate these obstacles?

How can you reduce the chances of them reoccurring?

How can these obstacles benefit you?

What mistakes did you make today?

What could you have done that would have been worse?

What can you do to mitigate these mistakes?

What could you do better next time?

What did you do well today?

What can you look forward to tomorrow?

Did you do what was appropriate to complete your tasks?	**YES / NO**
Did you complete your knockout list?	**YES / NO**
Are you closer to your goals today?	**YES / NO**
Did you behave according to your principles?	**YES / NO**

Fill in your Gratitude Log and 28 Day Tracking

Evening Reading:

Meditate ☐
(pg 217)

TUESDAY
MORNING PREPARATION
WEEK 1, DAY 2

How long did you sleep? Meditate ☐   Morning Reading:
(pg 216)

How well did you sleep? /5   Exercise ☐

Review your 7-day goals. With those goals in mind, make a **'Knockout List'** of 3-5 tasks you must work to complete today. Specify the tasks, and make them something you expect you can achieve today.

What are some likely preferred results if you complete these tasks?

What are some likely unpreferred results if you don't?

What is most in your control to complete these tasks?

What are some obstacles you are likely to face today?

What can you do to prepare for or reduce the chances of them happening?

What should you do if these obstacles happen?

> *"It does not matter what you bear, but how you bear it."*
> — *Seneca*

EVENING REVIEW

BREAKFAST	LUNCH	SUPPER	SNACKS

What were the most significant obstacles you faced today?

How could these obstacles have been worse?

How did you or how can you mitigate these obstacles?

How can you reduce the chances of them reoccurring?

How can these obstacles benefit you?

What mistakes did you make today?

What could you have done that would have been worse?

What can you do to mitigate these mistakes?

What could you do better next time?

What did you do well today?

What can you look forward to tomorrow?

Did you do what was appropriate to complete your tasks?	**YES / NO**
Did you complete your knockout list?	**YES / NO**
Are you closer to your goals today?	**YES / NO**
Did you behave according to your principles?	**YES / NO**

Fill in your Gratitude Log and 28 Day Tracking

Evening Reading:

Meditate ☐
(pg 217)

WEDNESDAY — WEEK 1, DAY 3
MORNING PREPARATION

How long did you sleep?   Meditate ☐   Morning Reading:
                                (pg 216)
How well did you sleep? /5   Exercise ☐

Review your 7-day goals. With those goals in mind, make a **'Knockout List'** of 3-5 tasks you must work to complete today. Specify the tasks, and make them something you expect you can achieve today.

What are some likely preferred results if you complete these tasks?

What are some likely unpreferred results if you don't?

What is most in your control to complete these tasks?

What are some obstacles you are likely to face today?

What can you do to prepare for or reduce the chances of them happening?

What should you do if these obstacles happen?

> *"Life is a shipwreck, but we must not forget to sing in the lifeboats."*
> — *Voltaire*

EVENING REVIEW

BREAKFAST	LUNCH	SUPPER	SNACKS

What were the most significant obstacles you faced today?

How could these obstacles have been worse?

How did you or how can you mitigate these obstacles?

How can you reduce the chances of them reoccurring?

How can these obstacles benefit you?

What mistakes did you make today?

What could you have done that would have been worse?

What can you do to mitigate these mistakes?

What could you do better next time?

What did you do well today?

What can you look forward to tomorrow?

Did you do what was appropriate to complete your tasks?	**YES / NO**
Did you complete your knockout list?	**YES / NO**
Are you closer to your goals today?	**YES / NO**
Did you behave according to your principles?	**YES / NO**

Fill in your Gratitude Log and 28 Day Tracking

Evening Reading:

Meditate ☐
(pg 217)

THURSDAY — WEEK 1, DAY 4
MORNING PREPARATION

How long did you sleep?   Meditate ☐ (pg 216)

How well did you sleep? /5   Exercise ☐

Morning Reading:

Review your 7-day goals. With those goals in mind, make a **'Knockout List'** of 3-5 tasks you must work to complete today. Specify the tasks, and make them something you expect you can achieve today.

What are some likely preferred results if you complete these tasks?

What are some likely unpreferred results if you don't?

What is most in your control to complete these tasks?

What are some obstacles you are likely to face today?

What can you do to prepare for or reduce the chances of them happening?

What should you do if these obstacles happen?

> "In the mean time, cling tooth and nail to the following rule: not to give in to adversity, not to trust prosperity, and always take full note of fortune's habit of behaving just as she pleases."
> - *Seneca*

EVENING REVIEW

BREAKFAST	LUNCH	SUPPER	SNACKS

What were the most significant obstacles you faced today?

How could these obstacles have been worse?

How did you or how can you mitigate these obstacles?

How can you reduce the chances of them reoccurring?

How can these obstacles benefit you?

What mistakes did you make today?

What could you have done that would have been worse?

What can you do to mitigate these mistakes?

What could you do better next time?

What did you do well today?

What can you look forward to tomorrow?

Did you do what was appropriate to complete your tasks?	**YES / NO**
Did you complete your knockout list?	**YES / NO**
Are you closer to your goals today?	**YES / NO**
Did you behave according to your principles?	**YES / NO**

Fill in your Gratitude Log and 28 Day Tracking

Evening Reading:

Meditate ☐
(pg 217)

FRIDAY   WEEK 1, DAY 5
MORNING PREPARATION

How long did you sleep?   Meditate ☐   Morning Reading:
(pg 216)

How well did you sleep? /5   Exercise ☐

Review your 7-day goals. With those goals in mind, make a **'Knockout List'** of 3-5 tasks you must work to complete today. Specify the tasks, and make them something you expect you can achieve today.

What are some likely preferred results if you complete these tasks?

What are some likely unpreferred results if you don't?

What is most in your control to complete these tasks?

What are some obstacles you are likely to face today?

What can you do to prepare for or reduce the chances of them happening?

What should you do if these obstacles happen?

> "There is only one way to happiness and that is to cease worrying about things which are beyond the power of our will."
> - Epictetus

EVENING REVIEW

BREAKFAST	LUNCH	SUPPER	SNACKS

What were the most significant obstacles you faced today?

How could these obstacles have been worse?

How did you or how can you mitigate these obstacles?

How can you reduce the chances of them reoccurring?

How can these obstacles benefit you?

What mistakes did you make today?

What could you have done that would have been worse?

What can you do to mitigate these mistakes?

What could you do better next time?

What did you do well today?

What can you look forward to tomorrow?

Did you do what was appropriate to complete your tasks?	**YES / NO**
Did you complete your knockout list?	**YES / NO**
Are you closer to your goals today?	**YES / NO**
Did you behave according to your principles?	**YES / NO**

Fill in your Gratitude Log and 28 Day Tracking

Evening Reading:

Meditate ☐
(pg 217)

SATURDAY
MORNING PREPARATION
WEEK 1, DAY 6

How long did you sleep?   Meditate ☐
(pg 216)

How well did you sleep? /5   Exercise ☐

Morning Reading:

Review your 7-day goals. With those goals in mind, make a **'Knockout List'** of 3-5 tasks you must work to complete today. Specify the tasks, and make them something you expect you can achieve today.

What are some likely preferred results if you complete these tasks?

What are some likely unpreferred results if you don't?

What is most in your control to complete these tasks?

What are some obstacles you are likely to face today?

What can you do to prepare for or reduce the chances of them happening?

What should you do if these obstacles happen?

> "The wise man is neither raised up by prosperity nor cast down by adversity; for always he has striven to rely predominantly on himself, and to derive all joy from himself."
> — Seneca

EVENING REVIEW

BREAKFAST	LUNCH	SUPPER	SNACKS

What were the most significant obstacles you faced today?

How could these obstacles have been worse?

How did you or how can you mitigate these obstacles?

How can you reduce the chances of them reoccurring?

How can these obstacles benefit you?

What mistakes did you make today?

What could you have done that would have been worse?

What can you do to mitigate these mistakes?

What could you do better next time?

What did you do well today?

What can you look forward to tomorrow?

Did you do what was appropriate to complete your tasks?	**YES / NO**
Did you complete your knockout list?	**YES / NO**
Are you closer to your goals today?	**YES / NO**
Did you behave according to your principles?	**YES / NO**

Fill in your Gratitude Log and 28 Day Tracking

Evening Reading:

Meditate ☐
(pg 217)

50

SUNDAY WEEK 1, DAY 7
MORNING PREPARATION

How long did you sleep? Meditate ☐ | Morning Reading:
(pg 216)

How well did you sleep? /5   Exercise ☐

Review your 7-day goals. With those goals in mind, make a **'Knockout List'** of 3-5 tasks you must work to complete today. Specify the tasks, and make them something you expect you can achieve today.

What are some likely preferred results if you complete these tasks?

What are some likely unpreferred results if you don't?

What is most in your control to complete these tasks?

What are some obstacles you are likely to face today?

What can you do to prepare for or reduce the chances of them happening?

What should you do if these obstacles happen?

> *Learn to be indifferent to what makes no difference.*
> — Marcus Aurelius

EVENING REVIEW

BREAKFAST	LUNCH	SUPPER	SNACKS

What were the most significant obstacles you faced today?

How could these obstacles have been worse?

How did you or how can you mitigate these obstacles?

How can you reduce the chances of them reoccurring?

How can these obstacles benefit you?

What mistakes did you make today?

What could you have done that would have been worse?

What can you do to mitigate these mistakes?

What could you do better next time?

What did you do well today?

What can you look forward to tomorrow?

Did you do what was appropriate to complete your tasks?	**YES / NO**
Did you complete your knockout list?	**YES / NO**
Are you closer to your goals today?	**YES / NO**
Did you behave according to your principles?	**YES / NO**

Fill in your Gratitude Log and 28 Day Tracking

Evening Reading:

Meditate ☐
(pg 217)

WEEK 1 GRATITUDE LOG

MONDAY

TUESDAY

WEDNESDAY

THURSDAY

FRIDAY

SATURDAY

SUNDAY

WEEK 1 REVIEW

○ Review your 7-day goals. Did you accopmlish them? **YES / NO** If no, consider why not, and if it is still worth your time. If it is, migrate it forward into a future task.

What were the best things that happened this week?

Which activities did not work well for you this week?

What activities worked well for you this week?

Overall, this week was:

WEEKLY PREMEDITATION OF OBSTACLES

Think of a significant obstacle happening to you, or think about suffering a significant loss. Imagine it as if it were happening now. Describe it in detail.

What would be the best way to react to this happening?

What are some things you now enjoy which you could no longer enjoy if this happens to you? Describe what you enjoy about it in detail.

How could you repair any damage caused if this happened?

What could you still enjoy in your life if this happened?

What could you do to prepare for or reduce the chances of this happening?

It's a possibility that this could happen to you. But it hasn't yet. What can you do to appreciate what you have now?

"Now is the time to get serious about living your ideals. How long can you afford to put off who you really want to be? Your nobler self cannot wait any longer. Put your principles into practice – now. Stop the excuses and the procrastination. This is your life! Decide to be extraordinary and do what you need to do – now."

- Epictetus

WEEKLY REFLECTION

7-DAY GOAL SETTING - WEEK 2

Review your 28-day goals. Look at the steps you should do to achieve the goals, and what you can do to reduce the chances of the obstacles you anticipated. With those in mind, what are your goals for the next 7 days? Make them specific and achievable in 7 days.

What are some likely preferred results if the goals are met?

What are some likely unpreferred results if the goals are not met?

What are the steps to take to most likely achieve the goals?

What are some obstacles that may obstruct meeting the goal?

What can you do to prepare for or reduce the chances of them happening?

What should you do if these obstacles happen?

WEEK 2 PLANNER

	Monday	Tuesday	Wednesday

	Thursday	Friday	Saturday	Sunday

MONDAY
MORNING PREPARATION
WEEK 2, DAY 1

How long did you sleep? ____   Meditate ☐ (pg 216)   Morning Reading:

How well did you sleep? __/5   Exercise ☐

Review your 7-day goals. With those goals in mind, make a **'Knockout List'** of 3-5 tasks you must work to complete today. Specify the tasks, and make them something you expect you can achieve today.

What are some likely preferred results if you complete these tasks?

What are some likely unpreferred results if you don't?

What is most in your control to complete these tasks?

What are some obstacles you are likely to face today?

What can you do to prepare for or reduce the chances of them happening?

What should you do if these obstacles happen?

> "Objective judgment, at this very moment. Unselfish action, now at this very moment. Willing acceptance – now at this very moment – of all external events. That's all you need."
> - *Marcus Aurelius*

EVENING REVIEW

BREAKFAST	LUNCH	SUPPER	SNACKS

What were the most significant obstacles you faced today?

How could these obstacles have been worse?

How did you or how can you mitigate these obstacles?

How can you reduce the chances of them reoccurring?

How can these obstacles benefit you?

What mistakes did you make today?

What could you have done that would have been worse?

What can you do to mitigate these mistakes?

What could you do better next time?

What did you do well today?

What can you look forward to tomorrow?

Did you do what was appropriate to complete your tasks?	**YES / NO**
Did you complete your knockout list?	**YES / NO**
Are you closer to your goals today?	**YES / NO**
Did you behave according to your principles?	**YES / NO**

Fill in your Gratitude Log and 28 Day Tracking

Evening Reading:

Meditate ☐
(pg 217)

TUESDAY   WEEK 2, DAY 2
MORNING PREPARATION

How long did you sleep?   Meditate ☐   Morning Reading:
(pg 216)

How well did you sleep? /5   Exercise ☐

Review your 7-day goals. With those goals in mind, make a **'Knockout List'** of 3-5 tasks you must work to complete today. Specify the tasks, and make them something you expect you can achieve today.

What are some likely preferred results if you complete these tasks?

What are some likely unpreferred results if you don't?

What is most in your control to complete these tasks?

What are some obstacles you are likely to face today?

What can you do to prepare for or reduce the chances of them happening?

What should you do if these obstacles happen?

> *Begin at once to live, and count each separate day as a separate life.*
> — *Seneca*

EVENING REVIEW

BREAKFAST	LUNCH	SUPPER	SNACKS

What were the most significant obstacles you faced today?

How could these obstacles have been worse?

How did you or how can you mitigate these obstacles?

How can you reduce the chances of them reoccurring?

How can these obstacles benefit you?

What mistakes did you make today?

What could you have done that would have been worse?

What can you do to mitigate these mistakes?

What could you do better next time?

What did you do well today?

What can you look forward to tomorrow?

Did you do what was appropriate to complete your tasks?	**YES / NO**
Did you complete your knockout list?	**YES / NO**
Are you closer to your goals today?	**YES / NO**
Did you behave according to your principles?	**YES / NO**

Fill in your Gratitude Log and 28 Day Tracking

Evening Reading:

Meditate ☐
(pg 217)

WEDNESDAY — WEEK 2, DAY 3
MORNING PREPARATION

How long did you sleep? Meditate ☐ | Morning Reading:
(pg 216)

How well did you sleep? /5   Exercise ☐

Review your 7-day goals. With those goals in mind, make a **'Knockout List'** of 3-5 tasks you must work to complete today. Specify the tasks, and make them something you expect you can achieve today.

What are some likely preferred results if you complete these tasks?

What are some likely unpreferred results if you don't?

What is most in your control to complete these tasks?

What are some obstacles you are likely to face today?

What can you do to prepare for or reduce the chances of them happening?

What should you do if these obstacles happen?

> "How long are you going to wait before you demand the best of yourself?"
> — *Epictetus*

EVENING REVIEW

BREAKFAST	LUNCH	SUPPER	SNACKS

What were the most significant obstacles you faced today?

How could these obstacles have been worse?

How did you or how can you mitigate these obstacles?

How can you reduce the chances of them reoccurring?

How can these obstacles benefit you?

What mistakes did you make today?

What could you have done that would have been worse?

What can you do to mitigate these mistakes?

What could you do better next time?

What did you do well today?

What can you look forward to tomorrow?

Did you do what was appropriate to complete your tasks?	**YES / NO**
Did you complete your knockout list?	**YES / NO**
Are you closer to your goals today?	**YES / NO**
Did you behave according to your principles?	**YES / NO**

◯ Fill in your Gratitude Log and 28 Day Tracking

Evening Reading:

Meditate ☐
(pg 217)

THURSDAY
MORNING PREPARATION
WEEK 2, DAY 4

How long did you sleep?　　　Meditate ☐
(pg 216)

How well did you sleep?　/5　Exercise ☐

Morning Reading:

Review your 7-day goals. With those goals in mind, make a **'Knockout List'** of 3-5 tasks you must work to complete today. Specify the tasks, and make them something you expect you can achieve today.

What are some likely preferred results if you complete these tasks?

What are some likely unpreferred results if you don't?

What is most in your control to complete these tasks?

What are some obstacles you are likely to face today?

What can you do to prepare for or reduce the chances of them happening?

What should you do if these obstacles happen?

> *"There is a limit to the time assigned you, and if you don't use it to free yourself it will be gone and will never return."*
>
> *- Marcus Aurelius*

EVENING REVIEW

BREAKFAST	LUNCH	SUPPER	SNACKS

What were the most significant obstacles you faced today?

How could these obstacles have been worse?

How did you or how can you mitigate these obstacles?

How can you reduce the chances of them reoccurring?

How can these obstacles benefit you?

What mistakes did you make today?

What could you have done that would have been worse?

What can you do to mitigate these mistakes?

What could you do better next time?

What did you do well today?

What can you look forward to tomorrow?

Did you do what was appropriate to complete your tasks?	**YES / NO**
Did you complete your knockout list?	**YES / NO**
Are you closer to your goals today?	**YES / NO**
Did you behave according to your principles?	**YES / NO**

◯ Fill in your Gratitude Log and 28 Day Tracking

Evening Reading:

Meditate ☐
(pg 217)

FRIDAY — MORNING PREPARATION
WEEK 2, DAY 5

How long did you sleep? Meditate ☐ (pg 216)

How well did you sleep? /5 Exercise ☐

Morning Reading:

Review your 7-day goals. With those goals in mind, make a **'Knockout List'** of 3-5 tasks you must work to complete today. Specify the tasks, and make them something you expect you can achieve today.

What are some likely preferred results if you complete these tasks?

What are some likely unpreferred results if you don't?

What is most in your control to complete these tasks?

What are some obstacles you are likely to face today?

What can you do to prepare for or reduce the chances of them happening?

What should you do if these obstacles happen?

> "Let us not postpone anything, let us engage in combats with life each day."
> — *Seneca*

EVENING REVIEW

BREAKFAST	LUNCH	SUPPER	SNACKS

What were the most significant obstacles you faced today?

How could these obstacles have been worse?

How did you or how can you mitigate these obstacles?

How can you reduce the chances of them reoccurring?

How can these obstacles benefit you?

What mistakes did you make today?

What could you have done that would have been worse?

What can you do to mitigate these mistakes?

What could you do better next time?

What did you do well today?

What can you look forward to tomorrow?

Did you do what was appropriate to complete your tasks?	**YES / NO**
Did you complete your knockout list?	**YES / NO**
Are you closer to your goals today?	**YES / NO**
Did you behave according to your principles?	**YES / NO**

Fill in your Gratitude Log and 28 Day Tracking

Evening Reading:

Meditate ☐
(pg 217)

SATURDAY
MORNING PREPARATION
WEEK 2, DAY 6

How long did you sleep? Meditate ☐
(pg 216)

How well did you sleep? /5 Exercise ☐

Morning Reading:

Review your 7-day goals. With those goals in mind, make a **'Knockout List'** of 3-5 tasks you must work to complete today. Specify the tasks, and make them something you expect you can achieve today.

What are some likely preferred results if you complete these tasks?

What are some likely unpreferred results if you don't?

What is most in your control to complete these tasks?

What are some obstacles you are likely to face today?

What can you do to prepare for or reduce the chances of them happening?

What should you do if these obstacles happen?

> *"While we wait for life, life passes."*
> — *Seneca*

EVENING REVIEW

BREAKFAST	LUNCH	SUPPER	SNACKS

What were the most significant obstacles you faced today?

How could these obstacles have been worse?

How did you or how can you mitigate these obstacles?

How can you reduce the chances of them reoccurring?

How can these obstacles benefit you?

What mistakes did you make today?

What could you have done that would have been worse?

What can you do to mitigate these mistakes?

What could you do better next time?

What did you do well today?

What can you look forward to tomorrow?

Did you do what was appropriate to complete your tasks?	**YES / NO**
Did you complete your knockout list?	**YES / NO**
Are you closer to your goals today?	**YES / NO**
Did you behave according to your principles?	**YES / NO**

Fill in your Gratitude Log and 28 Day Tracking

Evening Reading:

Meditate ☐
(pg 217)

SUNDAY — WEEK 2, DAY 7
MORNING PREPARATION

How long did you sleep?   Meditate ☐ (pg 216)   Morning Reading:

How well did you sleep? /5   Exercise ☐

Review your 7-day goals. With those goals in mind, make a **'Knockout List'** of 3-5 tasks you must work to complete today. Specify the tasks, and make them something you expect you can achieve today.

What are some likely preferred results if you complete these tasks?

What are some likely unpreferred results if you don't?

What is most in your control to complete these tasks?

What are some obstacles you are likely to face today?

What can you do to prepare for or reduce the chances of them happening?

What should you do if these obstacles happen?

> *"The whole future lies in uncertainty: live immediately."*
> — *Seneca*

EVENING REVIEW

BREAKFAST	LUNCH	SUPPER	SNACKS

What were the most significant obstacles you faced today?

How could these obstacles have been worse?

How did you or how can you mitigate these obstacles?

How can you reduce the chances of them reoccurring?

How can these obstacles benefit you?

What mistakes did you make today?

What could you have done that would have been worse?

What can you do to mitigate these mistakes?

What could you do better next time?

What did you do well today?

What can you look forward to tomorrow?

Did you do what was appropriate to complete your tasks?	**YES / NO**
Did you complete your knockout list?	**YES / NO**
Are you closer to your goals today?	**YES / NO**
Did you behave according to your principles?	**YES / NO**

Fill in your Gratitude Log and 28 Day Tracking

Evening Reading:

Meditate ☐
(pg 217)

105

WEEK 2 GRATITUDE LOG

MONDAY

TUESDAY

WEDNESDAY

THURSDAY

FRIDAY

SATURDAY

SUNDAY

WEEK 2 REVIEW

○ Review your 7-day goals. Did you accopmlish them? **YES / NO**
If no, consider why not, and if it is still worth your time. If it is, migrate it forward into a future task.

What were the best things that happened this week?

Which activities did not work well for you this week?

What activities worked well for you this week?

Overall, this week was:

WEEKLY PREMEDITATION OF OBSTACLES

Think of a significant obstacle happening to you, or think about suffering a significant loss. Imagine it as if it were happening now. Describe it in detail.

What would be the best way to react to this happening?

What are some things you now enjoy which you could no longer enjoy if this happens to you? Describe what you enjoy about it in detail.

How could you repair any damage caused if this happened?

What could you still enjoy in your life if this happened?

What could you do to prepare for or reduce the chances of this happening?

It's a possibility that this could happen to you. But it hasn't yet. What can you do to appreciate what you have now?

"Yes, you can — if you do everything as if it were the last thing you were doing in life, and stop being aimless, stop letting your emotions override what your mind tells you, stop being hypocritical, self-centered, irritable."

- Marcus Aurelius

WEEKLY REFLECTION

7-DAY GOAL SETTING - WEEK 3

Review your 28-day goals. Look at the steps you should do to achieve the goals, and what you can do to reduce the chances of the obstacles you anticipated. With those in mind, what are your goals for the next 7 days? Make them specific and achievable in 7 days.

What are some likely preferred results if the goals are met?

What are some likely unpreferred results if the goals are not met?

What are the steps to take to most likely achieve the goals?

What are some obstacles that may obstruct meeting the goal?

What can you do to prepare for or reduce the chances of them happening?

What should you do if these obstacles happen?

WEEK 3 PLANNER

	Monday	Tuesday	Wednesday

	Thursday	Friday	Saturday	Sunday

MONDAY WEEK 3, DAY 1
MORNING PREPARATION

How long did you sleep?   Meditate ☐ (pg 216)

How well did you sleep? /5   Exercise ☐

Morning Reading:

Review your 7-day goals. With those goals in mind, make a **'Knockout List'** of 3-5 tasks you must work to complete today. Specify the tasks, and make them something you expect you can achieve today.

What are some likely preferred results if you complete these tasks?

What are some likely unpreferred results if you don't?

What is most in your control to complete these tasks?

What are some obstacles you are likely to face today?

What can you do to prepare for or reduce the chances of them happening?

What should you do if these obstacles happen?

> *"Man conquers the world by conquering himself."*
> — Zeno of Citium

EVENING REVIEW

BREAKFAST	LUNCH	SUPPER	SNACKS

What were the most significant obstacles you faced today?

How could these obstacles have been worse?

How did you or how can you mitigate these obstacles?

How can you reduce the chances of them reoccurring?

How can these obstacles benefit you?

What mistakes did you make today?

What could you have done that would have been worse?

What can you do to mitigate these mistakes?

What could you do better next time?

What did you do well today?

What can you look forward to tomorrow?

Did you do what was appropriate to complete your tasks?	**YES / NO**
Did you complete your knockout list?	**YES / NO**
Are you closer to your goals today?	**YES / NO**
Did you behave according to your principles?	**YES / NO**

◯ Fill in your Gratitude Log and 28 Day Tracking

Evening Reading:

Meditate ☐
(pg 217)

TUESDAY
MORNING PREPARATION
WEEK 3, DAY 2

How long did you sleep?   Meditate ☐ (pg 216)

How well did you sleep? /5   Exercise ☐

Morning Reading:

Review your 7-day goals. With those goals in mind, make a **'Knockout List'** of 3-5 tasks you must work to complete today. Specify the tasks, and make them something you expect you can achieve today.

What are some likely preferred results if you complete these tasks?

What are some likely unpreferred results if you don't?

What is most in your control to complete these tasks?

What are some obstacles you are likely to face today?

What can you do to prepare for or reduce the chances of them happening?

What should you do if these obstacles happen?

> "To be evenminded is the greatest virtue."
> — *Heraclitus*

EVENING REVIEW

BREAKFAST	LUNCH	SUPPER	SNACKS

What were the most significant obstacles you faced today?

How could these obstacles have been worse?

How did you or how can you mitigate these obstacles?

How can you reduce the chances of them reoccurring?

How can these obstacles benefit you?

What mistakes did you make today?

What could you have done that would have been worse?

What can you do to mitigate these mistakes?

What could you do better next time?

What did you do well today?

What can you look forward to tomorrow?

Did you do what was appropriate to complete your tasks?	**YES / NO**
Did you complete your knockout list?	**YES / NO**
Are you closer to your goals today?	**YES / NO**
Did you behave according to your principles?	**YES / NO**

Fill in your Gratitude Log and 28 Day Tracking

Evening Reading:

Meditate ☐
(pg 217)

WEDNESDAY
MORNING PREPARATION
WEEK 3, DAY 3

How long did you sleep? Meditate ☐
(pg 216)

How well did you sleep? /5 Exercise ☐

Morning Reading:

Review your 7-day goals. With those goals in mind, make a **'Knockout List'** of 3-5 tasks you must work to complete today. Specify the tasks, and make them something you expect you can achieve today.

What are some likely preferred results if you complete these tasks?

What are some likely unpreferred results if you don't?

What is most in your control to complete these tasks?

What are some obstacles you are likely to face today?

What can you do to prepare for or reduce the chances of them happening?

What should you do if these obstacles happen?

> *"The true hero is one who conquers his own anger and hatred."*
> — *Dalai Lama*

EVENING REVIEW

BREAKFAST	LUNCH	SUPPER	SNACKS

What were the most significant obstacles you faced today?

How could these obstacles have been worse?

How did you or how can you mitigate these obstacles?

How can you reduce the chances of them reoccurring?

How can these obstacles benefit you?

What mistakes did you make today?

What could you have done that would have been worse?

What can you do to mitigate these mistakes?

What could you do better next time?

What did you do well today?

What can you look forward to tomorrow?

Did you do what was appropriate to complete your tasks?	**YES / NO**
Did you complete your knockout list?	**YES / NO**
Are you closer to your goals today?	**YES / NO**
Did you behave according to your principles?	**YES / NO**

Fill in your Gratitude Log and 28 Day Tracking

Evening Reading:

Meditate ☐
(pg 217)

THURSDAY
MORNING PREPARATION
WEEK 3, DAY 4

How long did you sleep?   Meditate ☐   Morning Reading:
(pg 216)

How well did you sleep? /5   Exercise ☐

Review your 7-day goals. With those goals in mind, make a **'Knockout List'** of 3-5 tasks you must work to complete today. Specify the tasks, and make them something you expect you can achieve today.

What are some likely preferred results if you complete these tasks?

What are some likely unpreferred results if you don't?

What is most in your control to complete these tasks?

What are some obstacles you are likely to face today?

What can you do to prepare for or reduce the chances of them happening?

What should you do if these obstacles happen?

> "No man is free who is not master of himself."
> — *Epictetus*

EVENING REVIEW

BREAKFAST	LUNCH	SUPPER	SNACKS

What were the most significant obstacles you faced today?

How could these obstacles have been worse?

How did you or how can you mitigate these obstacles?

How can you reduce the chances of them reoccurring?

How can these obstacles benefit you?

What mistakes did you make today?

What could you have done that would have been worse?

What can you do to mitigate these mistakes?

What could you do better next time?

What did you do well today?

What can you look forward to tomorrow?

Did you do what was appropriate to complete your tasks?	**YES / NO**
Did you complete your knockout list?	**YES / NO**
Are you closer to your goals today?	**YES / NO**
Did you behave according to your principles?	**YES / NO**

Fill in your Gratitude Log and 28 Day Tracking

Evening Reading:

Meditate ☐
(pg 217)

FRIDAY — MORNING PREPARATION
WEEK 3, DAY 5

How long did you sleep?   Meditate ☐ (pg 216)   Morning Reading:

How well did you sleep? /5   Exercise ☐

Review your 7-day goals. With those goals in mind, make a **'Knockout List'** of 3-5 tasks you must work to complete today. Specify the tasks, and make them something you expect you can achieve today.

What are some likely preferred results if you complete these tasks?

What are some likely unpreferred results if you don't?

What is most in your control to complete these tasks?

What are some obstacles you are likely to face today?

What can you do to prepare for or reduce the chances of them happening?

What should you do if these obstacles happen?

> "This is the mark of perfection of character - to spend each day as if it were your last, without frenzy, laziness, or any pretending."
> - Marcus Aurelius

EVENING REVIEW

BREAKFAST	LUNCH	SUPPER	SNACKS

What were the most significant obstacles you faced today?

How could these obstacles have been worse?

How did you or how can you mitigate these obstacles?

How can you reduce the chances of them reoccurring?

How can these obstacles benefit you?

What mistakes did you make today?

What could you have done that would have been worse?

What can you do to mitigate these mistakes?

What could you do better next time?

What did you do well today?

What can you look forward to tomorrow?

Did you do what was appropriate to complete your tasks?	**YES / NO**
Did you complete your knockout list?	**YES / NO**
Are you closer to your goals today?	**YES / NO**
Did you behave according to your principles?	**YES / NO**

Fill in your Gratitude Log and 28 Day Tracking

Evening Reading:

Meditate ☐
(pg 217)

SATURDAY
MORNING PREPARATION
WEEK 3, DAY 6

How long did you sleep?   Meditate ☐   Morning Reading:
(pg 216)
How well did you sleep? /5   Exercise ☐

Review your 7-day goals. With those goals in mind, make a **'Knockout List'** of 3-5 tasks you must work to complete today. Specify the tasks, and make them something you expect you can achieve today.

What are some likely preferred results if you complete these tasks?

What are some likely unpreferred results if you don't?

What is most in your control to complete these tasks?

What are some obstacles you are likely to face today?

What can you do to prepare for or reduce the chances of them happening?

What should you do if these obstacles happen?

> *"Progress is not achieved by luck or accident, but by working on yourself daily."*
> — *Epictetus*

EVENING REVIEW

BREAKFAST	LUNCH	SUPPER	SNACKS

What were the most significant obstacles you faced today?

How could these obstacles have been worse?

How did you or how can you mitigate these obstacles?

How can you reduce the chances of them reoccurring?

How can these obstacles benefit you?

What mistakes did you make today?

What could you have done that would have been worse?

What can you do to mitigate these mistakes?

What could you do better next time?

What did you do well today?

What can you look forward to tomorrow?

Did you do what was appropriate to complete your tasks?	**YES / NO**
Did you complete your knockout list?	**YES / NO**
Are you closer to your goals today?	**YES / NO**
Did you behave according to your principles?	**YES / NO**

Fill in your Gratitude Log and 28 Day Tracking

Evening Reading:

Meditate ☐
(pg 217)

SUNDAY
MORNING PREPARATION
WEEK 3, DAY 7

How long did you sleep? Meditate ☐
(pg 216)
How well did you sleep? /5 Exercise ☐

Morning Reading:

Review your 7-day goals. With those goals in mind, make a **'Knockout List'** of 3-5 tasks you must work to complete today. Specify the tasks, and make them something you expect you can achieve today.

What are some likely preferred results if you complete these tasks?

What are some likely unpreferred results if you don't?

What is most in your control to complete these tasks?

What are some obstacles you are likely to face today?

What can you do to prepare for or reduce the chances of them happening?

What should you do if these obstacles happen?

> "If you accomplish something good with hard work, the labor passes quickly, but the good endures; if you do something shameful in pursuit of pleasure, the pleasure passes quickly, but the shame endures."
> — Musonius Rufus

EVENING REVIEW

BREAKFAST	LUNCH	SUPPER	SNACKS

What were the most significant obstacles you faced today?

. . . .

. . . .

. . . .

How could these obstacles have been worse?

. . . .

. . . .

. . . .

How did you or how can you mitigate these obstacles?

. . . .

. . . .

. . . .

How can you reduce the chances of them reoccurring?

. . . .

. . . .

. . . .

How can these obstacles benefit you?

. . . .

. . . .

. . . .

What mistakes did you make today?

What could you have done that would have been worse?

What can you do to mitigate these mistakes?

What could you do better next time?

What did you do well today?

What can you look forward to tomorrow?

Did you do what was appropriate to complete your tasks?	**YES / NO**
Did you complete your knockout list?	**YES / NO**
Are you closer to your goals today?	**YES / NO**
Did you behave according to your principles?	**YES / NO**

Fill in your Gratitude Log and 28 Day Tracking

Evening Reading:

Meditate ☐
(pg 217)

150

WEEK 3 GRATITUDE LOG

MONDAY

TUESDAY

WEDNESDAY

THURSDAY

FRIDAY

SATURDAY

SUNDAY

WEEK 3 REVIEW

◯ Review your 7-day goals. Did you accopmlish them? **YES / NO** If no, consider why not, and if it is still worth your time. If it is, migrate it forward into a future task.

What were the best things that happened this week?

Which activities did not work well for you this week?

What activities worked well for you this week?

Overall, this week was:

WEEKLY PREMEDITATION OF OBSTACLES

Think of a significant obstacle happening to you, or think about suffering a significant loss. Imagine it as if it were happening now. Describe it in detail.

What would be the best way to react to this happening?

What are some things you now enjoy which you could no longer enjoy if this happens to you? Describe what you enjoy about it in detail.

How could you repair any damage caused if this happened?

What could you still enjoy in your life if this happened?

What could you do to prepare for or reduce the chances of this happening?

It's a possibility that this could happen to you. But it hasn't yet. What can you do to appreciate what you have now?

> "Just that you do the right thing. The rest doesn't matter. Cold or warm. Tired or well-rested. Despised or honored. Dying... or busy with other assignments."
>
> – Marcus Aurelius

WEEKLY REFLECTION

7-DAY GOAL SETTING - WEEK 4

Review your 28-day goals. Look at the steps you should do to achieve the goals, and what you can do to reduce the chances of the obstacles you anticipated. With those in mind, what are your goals for the next 7 days? Make them specific and achievable in 7 days.

What are some likely preferred results if the goals are met?

What are some likely unpreferred results if the goals are not met?

What are the steps to take to most likely achieve the goals?

What are some obstacles that may obstruct meeting the goal?

What can you do to prepare for or reduce the chances of them happening?

What should you do if these obstacles happen?

WEEK 4 PLANNER

	Monday	Tuesday	Wednesday

	Thursday	Friday	Saturday	Sunday

MONDAY WEEK 4, DAY 1
MORNING PREPARATION

How long did you sleep?   Meditate ☐   Morning Reading:
(pg 216)

How well did you sleep? /5   Exercise ☐

Review your 7-day goals. With those goals in mind, make a **'Knockout List'** of 3-5 tasks you must work to complete today. Specify the tasks, and make them something you expect you can achieve today.

What are some likely preferred results if you complete these tasks?

What are some likely unpreferred results if you don't?

What is most in your control to complete these tasks?

What are some obstacles you are likely to face today?

What can you do to prepare for or reduce the chances of them happening?

What should you do if these obstacles happen?

> "The first rule is to keep an untroubled spirit. The second is to look things in the face and know them for what they are."
> *- Marcus Aurelius*

EVENING REVIEW

BREAKFAST	LUNCH	SUPPER	SNACKS

What were the most significant obstacles you faced today?

How could these obstacles have been worse?

How did you or how can you mitigate these obstacles?

How can you reduce the chances of them reoccurring?

How can these obstacles benefit you?

What mistakes did you make today?

What could you have done that would have been worse?

What can you do to mitigate these mistakes?

What could you do better next time?

What did you do well today?

What can you look forward to tomorrow?

Did you do what was appropriate to complete your tasks?	**YES / NO**
Did you complete your knockout list?	**YES / NO**
Are you closer to your goals today?	**YES / NO**
Did you behave according to your principles?	**YES / NO**

Fill in your Gratitude Log and 28 Day Tracking

Evening Reading:

Meditate ☐
(pg 217)

TUESDAY
MORNING PREPARATION
WEEK 4, DAY 2

How long did you sleep? Meditate ☐
(pg 216)

How well did you sleep? /5 Exercise ☐

Morning Reading:

Review your 7-day goals. With those goals in mind, make a **'Knockout List'** of 3-5 tasks you must work to complete today. Specify the tasks, and make them something you expect you can achieve today.

What are some likely preferred results if you complete these tasks?

What are some likely unpreferred results if you don't?

What is most in your control to complete these tasks?

What are some obstacles you are likely to face today?

What can you do to prepare for or reduce the chances of them happening?

What should you do if these obstacles happen?

> *"The secret of happiness, you see, is not found in seeking more, but in developing the capacity to enjoy less."*
> — *Socrates*

EVENING REVIEW

BREAKFAST	LUNCH	SUPPER	SNACKS

What were the most significant obstacles you faced today?

How could these obstacles have been worse?

How did you or how can you mitigate these obstacles?

How can you reduce the chances of them reoccurring?

How can these obstacles benefit you?

What mistakes did you make today?

What could you have done that would have been worse?

What can you do to mitigate these mistakes?

What could you do better next time?

What did you do well today?

What can you look forward to tomorrow?

Did you do what was appropriate to complete your tasks?	**YES / NO**
Did you complete your knockout list?	**YES / NO**
Are you closer to your goals today?	**YES / NO**
Did you behave according to your principles?	**YES / NO**

Fill in your Gratitude Log and 28 Day Tracking

Evening Reading:

Meditate ☐
(pg 217)

WEDNESDAY
MORNING PREPARATION
WEEK 4, DAY 3

How long did you sleep? Meditate ☐ Morning Reading:
(pg 216)

How well did you sleep? /5 Exercise ☐

Review your 7-day goals. With those goals in mind, make a **'Knockout List'** of 3-5 tasks you must work to complete today. Specify the tasks, and make them something you expect you can achieve today.

What are some likely preferred results if you complete these tasks?

What are some likely unpreferred results if you don't?

What is most in your control to complete these tasks?

What are some obstacles you are likely to face today?

What can you do to prepare for or reduce the chances of them happening?

What should you do if these obstacles happen?

> *"The tranquility that comes when you stop caring what they say. Or think, or do. Only what you do."*
> — *Marcus Aurelius*

EVENING REVIEW

BREAKFAST	LUNCH	SUPPER	SNACKS

What were the most significant obstacles you faced today?

How could these obstacles have been worse?

How did you or how can you mitigate these obstacles?

How can you reduce the chances of them reoccurring?

How can these obstacles benefit you?

What mistakes did you make today?

What could you have done that would have been worse?

What can you do to mitigate these mistakes?

What could you do better next time?

What did you do well today?

What can you look forward to tomorrow?

Did you do what was appropriate to complete your tasks?	**YES / NO**
Did you complete your knockout list?	**YES / NO**
Are you closer to your goals today?	**YES / NO**
Did you behave according to your principles?	**YES / NO**

Fill in your Gratitude Log and 28 Day Tracking

Evening Reading:

Meditate ☐
(pg 217)

THURSDAY
MORNING PREPARATION
WEEK 4, DAY 4

How long did you sleep? Meditate ☐   Morning Reading:
(pg 216)

How well did you sleep? /5   Exercise ☐

Review your 7-day goals. With those goals in mind, make a **'Knockout List'** of 3-5 tasks you must work to complete today. Specify the tasks, and make them something you expect you can achieve today.

What are some likely preferred results if you complete these tasks?

What are some likely unpreferred results if you don't?

What is most in your control to complete these tasks?

What are some obstacles you are likely to face today?

What can you do to prepare for or reduce the chances of them happening?

What should you do if these obstacles happen?

> "You will be attacked for doing the right thing. Do it anyway."

EVENING REVIEW

BREAKFAST	LUNCH	SUPPER	SNACKS

What were the most significant obstacles you faced today?

How could these obstacles have been worse?

How did you or how can you mitigate these obstacles?

How can you reduce the chances of them reoccurring?

How can these obstacles benefit you?

What mistakes did you make today?

What could you have done that would have been worse?

What can you do to mitigate these mistakes?

What could you do better next time?

What did you do well today?

What can you look forward to tomorrow?

Did you do what was appropriate to complete your tasks?	**YES / NO**
Did you complete your knockout list?	**YES / NO**
Are you closer to your goals today?	**YES / NO**
Did you behave according to your principles?	**YES / NO**

Fill in your Gratitude Log and 28 Day Tracking

Evening Reading:

Meditate ☐
(pg 217)

FRIDAY
MORNING PREPARATION
WEEK 4, DAY 5

How long did you sleep?   Meditate ☐   Morning Reading:
(pg 216)

How well did you sleep? /5   Exercise ☐

Review your 7-day goals. With those goals in mind, make a **'Knockout List'** of 3-5 tasks you must work to complete today. Specify the tasks, and make them something you expect you can achieve today.

What are some likely preferred results if you complete these tasks?

What are some likely unpreferred results if you don't?

What is most in your control to complete these tasks?

What are some obstacles you are likely to face today?

What can you do to prepare for or reduce the chances of them happening?

What should you do if these obstacles happen?

> "He who does not desire or fear the uncertain day or capricious fate, is equal to the gods above and loftier than mortals."
> - *Justus Lipsius*

EVENING REVIEW

BREAKFAST	LUNCH	SUPPER	SNACKS

What were the most significant obstacles you faced today?

How could these obstacles have been worse?

How did you or how can you mitigate these obstacles?

How can you reduce the chances of them reoccurring?

How can these obstacles benefit you?

What mistakes did you make today?

What could you have done that would have been worse?

What can you do to mitigate these mistakes?

What could you do better next time?

What did you do well today?

What can you look forward to tomorrow?

Did you do what was appropriate to complete your tasks?	**YES / NO**
Did you complete your knockout list?	**YES / NO**
Are you closer to your goals today?	**YES / NO**
Did you behave according to your principles?	**YES / NO**

Fill in your Gratitude Log and 28 Day Tracking

Evening Reading:

Meditate ☐
(pg 217)

SATURDAY — WEEK 4, DAY 6
MORNING PREPARATION

How long did you sleep?　　Meditate ☐　　| Morning Reading:
(pg 216)

How well did you sleep?　/5　Exercise ☐　|

Review your 7-day goals. With those goals in mind, make a **'Knockout List'** of 3-5 tasks you must work to complete today. Specify the tasks, and make them something you expect you can achieve today.

What are some likely preferred results if you complete these tasks?

What are some likely unpreferred results if you don't?

What is most in your control to complete these tasks?

What are some obstacles you are likely to face today?

What can you do to prepare for or reduce the chances of them happening?

What should you do if these obstacles happen?

> "You could leave life right now. Let that determine what you do and say and think."
> — *Marcus Aurelius*

EVENING REVIEW

BREAKFAST	LUNCH	SUPPER	SNACKS

What were the most significant obstacles you faced today?

How could these obstacles have been worse?

How did you or how can you mitigate these obstacles?

How can you reduce the chances of them reoccurring?

How can these obstacles benefit you?

What mistakes did you make today?

What could you have done that would have been worse?

What can you do to mitigate these mistakes?

What could you do better next time?

What did you do well today?

What can you look forward to tomorrow?

Did you do what was appropriate to complete your tasks?	**YES / NO**
Did you complete your knockout list?	**YES / NO**
Are you closer to your goals today?	**YES / NO**
Did you behave according to your principles?	**YES / NO**

◯ Fill in your Gratitude Log and 28 Day Tracking

Evening Reading:

Meditate ☐
(pg 217)

SUNDAY
MORNING PREPARATION
WEEK 4, DAY 7

How long did you sleep? Meditate ☐ Morning Reading:
(pg 216)

How well did you sleep? /5 Exercise ☐

Review your 7-day goals. With those goals in mind, make a **'Knockout List'** of 3-5 tasks you must work to complete today. Specify the tasks, and make them something you expect you can achieve today.

What are some likely preferred results if you complete these tasks?

What are some likely unpreferred results if you don't?

What is most in your control to complete these tasks?

What are some obstacles you are likely to face today?

What can you do to prepare for or reduce the chances of them happening?

What should you do if these obstacles happen?

> *"Not to assume it's impossible because you find it hard. But to recognize that if it's humanly possible, you can do it too."*
> — Marcus Aurelius

EVENING REVIEW

BREAKFAST	LUNCH	SUPPER	SNACKS

What were the most significant obstacles you faced today?

How could these obstacles have been worse?

How did you or how can you mitigate these obstacles?

How can you reduce the chances of them reoccurring?

How can these obstacles benefit you?

What mistakes did you make today?

What could you have done that would have been worse?

What can you do to mitigate these mistakes?

What could you do better next time?

What did you do well today?

What can you look forward to tomorrow?

Did you do what was appropriate to complete your tasks?	**YES / NO**
Did you complete your knockout list?	**YES / NO**
Are you closer to your goals today?	**YES / NO**
Did you behave according to your principles?	**YES / NO**

Fill in your Gratitude Log and 28 Day Tracking

Evening Reading:

Meditate ☐
(pg 217)

200

WEEK 4 GRATITUDE LOG

MONDAY

TUESDAY

WEDNESDAY

THURSDAY

FRIDAY

SATURDAY

SUNDAY

WEEK 4 REVIEW

○ Review your 7-day goals. Did you accopmlish them? **YES / NO** If no, consider why not, and if it is still worth your time. If it is, migrate it forward into a future task.

What were the best things that happened this week?

Which activities did not work well for you this week?

What activities worked well for you this week?

Overall, this week was:

205

WEEKLY PREMEDITATION OF OBSTACLES

Think of a significant obstacle happening to you, or think about suffering a significant loss. Imagine it as if it were happening now. Describe it in detail.

What would be the best way to react to this happening?

What are some things you now enjoy which you could no longer enjoy if this happens to you? Describe what you enjoy about it in detail.

How could you repair any damage caused if this happened?

What could you still enjoy in your life if this happened?

What could you do to prepare for or reduce the chances of this happening?

It's a possibility that this could happen to you. But it hasn't yet. What can you do to appreciate what you have now?

208

28 DAY TRACKING

28 DAY REVIEW

○ Review your 28-day goals. Did you accopmlish them? **YES / NO**
If no, consider why not, and if it is still worth your time. If it is, migrate it forward into a future task.

What were the best things that happened these last four weeks?

Which activities did not work well for you these last four weeks?

What activities worked well for you these last four weeks?

HEALTH & WELLNESS REVIEW

	CURRENT	CHANGE	TARGET
Weight			
Body Fat %			
Neck			
Shoulders			
Chest			
Right Bicep			
Left Bicep			
Right Forearm			
Left Forearm			
Waist			
Hips			
Right Thigh			
Left Thigh			
Right Calf			
Left Calf			
Push-ups in 60 seconds			
Pull-ups/Flex Arm Hang			
Squats in 60 seconds			
Sit-ups in 60 seconds			
Sit & Reach Distance			
12 Minute Run Distance			
Pulse before run			
Pulse after run			

On average for the last 4 weeks, how much do you agree?
On a scale of 1-10 with 1 being least agreement and 10 being most agreement

		CURRENT	CHANGE
PHYSICAL HEALTH	I am clean and orderly		
	I am sleeping well		
	I am exercising well		
	I feel properly energetic		
	Total Physical Health Score:		
EMOTIONAL HEALTH	I am not feeling worried or anxious		
	I am able to relax		
	I feel a sense of tranquility		
	I am not easily annoyed or irritated		
	Total Emotional Health Score:		
INTELLECTUAL HEALTH	I am consistently learning		
	I can consider ideas that I disagree with		
	I can change my opinion when appropriate		
	I am intellectually challenged		
	Total Intellectual Health Score:		
SPIRITUAL HEALTH	I can forgive myself and others		
	I feel a strong purpose in my life		
	I accept what I cannot change		
	I practice routines to develop my spirit		
	Total Spiritual Health Score:		
SOCIAL HEALTH	I don't feel lonely		
	I enjoy spending time with others		
	I make a positive contribution to my community		
	I do not attempt to avoid people		
	Total Social Health Score:		

Total Score:		Change:	

MORNING MEDITATION

1 - Zazen Breathing Meditation

2 - Wabi-Sabi Meditation

3 - Gratitude Meditation

4 - Adversity Meditation

5 - Agape Meditation

EVENING MEDITATION

1 - Zazen Breathing Meditation

2 - Wabi-Sabi Meditation

3 - Gratitude Meditation

4 - Forgiveness Meditation

5 - Agape Meditation

ZAZEN MEDITATION

Minutes of Zazen Breathing Meditation

Have a few minutes of quiet sitting to clear your mind of distractions.

Assume a comfortable seated position and keep your back straight.

Hold your head in a comfortable position, with your head aligned with your straight back, and your chin tucked in slightly.

Focus your eyes just ahead of you, either at a wall or at the floor. Keep your eyes slightly closed

Try not to think of anything at all, except perhaps your breath.

Try to expand your belly more than your chest as you breathe in through your nose.

Hold your breath slightly and only without any strain.

Breathe out through your nose.

Pay attention to rhythm and sound of your breathing. Feel the air entering and exiting your lungs. Strive to be as aware as possible of your breathing for the duration of your meditation.

If you start to think of anything other than your breath, bring your thoughts back to focus on your breath alone. If this is difficult, you can count your breaths until you no longer need to in order to keep your thoughts on your breath.

When learning Zazen, start with a 2 minute session. Increase that duration as your skill increases. A 7 minute session should be sufficient to clear your thoughts for the rest of your Stoic meditation.

WABI-SABI MEDITATION

Consider how the things in your life are imperfect, impermanent, and incomplete. See the beauty in this.

Nothing lasts, nothing is finished, and nothing is perfect.

Everything and everyone is imperfect. I have flaws and imperfections, as does everyone else. This is part of what we are and what makes us unique. There is beauty in the imperfections.

Everything and everyone is impermanent. Nothing stays the same. Nothing lasts forever. Change is the only constant. There is nothing we can really hold on to. These moments will never happen again. There is beauty in the impermanence.

Everything and everyone is incomplete. The world is a work in progress. You are a work in progress. There is beauty in this process of becoming.

GRATITUDE MEDITATION

No day is guaranteed to me. But today I am alive and air fills my lungs. For this, I am grateful.

I have consciousness. I have reason. For this, I am grateful.

I know very little, but I am not finished learning. For this, I am grateful.

I am not perfect, but I am not finished growing. For this, I am grateful.

My past is gone. I can start life anew today. For this, I am grateful.

I have the capacity to be virtuous, and virtue is sufficient for happiness. For this, I am grateful.

I don't need anything outside of myself to be content. For this, I am grateful.

I am able to be good. I am able to love. For this, I am grateful.

I am at peace. I am free. For this, I am grateful.

I cannot control what happens to me. But I can control how I react. For this, I am grateful.

With every trial, I am able to learn a lesson. For this, I am grateful.

With every hardship, I am able to respond with good. For this, I am grateful.

I can choose to forgive. For this, I am grateful.

The universe follows an order. Everything happens as it should. For this, I am grateful.

Everything is interwoven. I am a part of the divine. For this, I am grateful.

I am the universe, living briefly as a human. For this, I am grateful.

I will return to the universe and live on as it does. For this, I am grateful.

ADVERSITY MEDITATION

Remember, today you will face adversity

People I deal with today will be meddling, ungrateful, arrogant, dishonest, malicious, bitter, resentful, vindictive, jealous, and surly. They are like this because they confuse good and evil.

But I have seen the beauty of good, and the ugliness of evil, and have recognized that the wrongdoer has a nature kindred to my own - not of the same blood and birth, but the same mind, the same humanity, and possessing a share of the divine.

No wrongdoer can harm me. No one can bring me into evil. Nor can I feel angry at my kindred, or hate them. We were born to work together like feet, hands and eyes, like the two rows of teeth, upper and lower. To obstruct each other is deviant. To feel anger at someone, to turn your back on him: these are deviant.

FORGIVENESS MEDITATION

Forgive yourself and others for mistakes

If I have failed or harmed anyone in any way either knowingly or unknowingly, it was due to my own confusions; I ask their forgiveness.

If anyone has failed or harmed me in any way either knowingly or unknowingly, it was due to their own confusions; I forgive them.

For all the ways that I fail or harm myself, negate, doubt, belittle myself, judge or be unkind to myself, and for all the ways I fail to act according to my own principles, it is due to my own confusions; I forgive myself.

And if there is a situation I am not yet ready to forgive, it is due to my own confusions; I forgive myself for that.

AGAPE MEDITATION

A meditation for an unconditional, cosmopolitan love for all.

In this meditation you will wish well for yourself, and wish for others as you wish for yourself.

- **Love yourself.** Think of yourself and say:

> *I am important. I matter. I am precious. I am good.*
>
> *May I be at peace. May I be content and of a good spirit.*
>
> *May I be prosperous.*
>
> *May I want for nothing, suffer no misfortune, and live a good life.*

- **Love your family and friends.** Now imagine your friends and family, and say for them:

> *You are important. You matter. You are precious. You are good.*
>
> *May you be at peace. May you be content and of a good spirit.*
>
> *May you be prosperous.*
>
> *May you want for nothing, suffer no misfortune, and live a good life.*

- **Love your neighbours.** Think of someone you know who is not a friend or family, and say the same for them.

- **Love your enemies.** Think of someone who has done you wrong, or dislikes you, or even wishes you harm, and say the same for them.

- **Love all of mankind.** Imagine the people you haven't met - all of humanity - and say the same for them.

224

225

The Focused Stoic Journal 28 Day Undated Edition by Jeff Rout

Published by Domino Effect Publishing

© 2020 Jeff Rout

All rights reserved. No portion of this book may be reproduced in any form without permission from the publisher, except as permitted by Canadian and/or U.S. copyright law.

Cover by Jeff Rout

ISBN: 978-0-9867593-7-6

www.ingramcontent.com/pod-product-compliance
Lightning Source LLC
Chambersburg PA
CBHW020107020526
44112CB00033B/1089